Reading Together

THE STORY OF CHICKEN LICKEN

Read it together

The Story of Chicken Licken introduces children to a new way of storytelling – written down as a school play using speech bubbles.

Children enjoy joining in with the reading, pointing to the words as *you* read, and talking through the book afterwards. These are all signs that they are interested and want to find out more.

One of the most important ways you can help your child to be a reader is by reading aloud. Read aloud as often as you can – new stories and old favourites!

Children may notice the different kinds of pictures in this book. You might talk together about the way the audience is illustrated in silhouettes.

A developing interest in words and letters helps children learning to read. See if they can find words they recognize and similarities between words on the page. You can help them to write familiar words.

Now we need an "f" for fox.

If they are reading and get stuck on a word, you can show children how to guess what it might be by using the pictures or looking at the letter the word begins with. Always help them out if they're really stuck or tired.

One day Chicken L–

Licken.

I like all these shadow pictures here.

The pictures in this book tell more than the words. You can talk together about the baby's adventure or imagine what members of the audience are saying.

What do you think he's whispering to her?

We hope you enjoy reading this book together.

First published 1985
by Walker Books Ltd
87 Vauxhall Walk
London SE11 5HJ

This edition published 1998

6 8 10 9 7

© 1985 Jan Ormerod
Introductory and concluding notes
© 1998 CLPE/LB Southwark

Printed in Hong Kong

ISBN 0-7445-5704-6

OH, COCK LOCK, DON'T GO!
I was going and I met Chicken
Licken and the sky had fallen
on her poor little head.
Now we are going to tell the king.

OH, DUCK LUCK, DON'T GO!

I was going and I met Henny Penny,

and Henny Penny met Chicken Licken

and the sky had fallen

on her poor little head.

Now we are going to tell the king.

OH, DRAKE LAKE, DON'T GO!
I was going and I met Cock Lock,
and Cock Lock met Henny Penny,
and Henny Penny met Chicken Licken
and the sky had fallen
on her poor little head.
Now we are going to tell the king.

OH, GOOSE LOOSE, DON'T GO!

I was going and I met Duck Luck,

and Duck Luck met Cock Lock,

and Cock Lock met Henny Penny,

and Henny Penny met Chicken Licken

and the sky had fallen

on her poor little head.

Now we are going to tell the king.

OH, GANDER LANDER, DON'T GO!

I was going and I met Drake Lake,

and Drake Lake met Duck Luck,

and Duck Luck met Cock Lock,

and Cock Lock met Henny Penny,

and Henny Penny met Chicken Licken

and the sky had fallen

on her poor little head.

Now we are going to tell the king.

So Gander Lander turned back
and met Turkey Lurkey.
He asked Turkey Lurkey
where he was going.

I am going
to the woods
for some food.

OH, TURKEY LURKEY, DON'T GO!
I was going and I met Goose Loose,
and Goose Loose met Drake Lake,
and Drake Lake met Duck Luck,
and Duck Luck met Cock Lock,
and Cock Lock met Henny Penny,
and Henny Penny met
Chicken Licken and the sky
had fallen on her poor little head.
Now we are going to tell the king.

So Turkey Lurkey turned back
and walked with Gander Lander,
Goose Loose, Drake Lake,
Duck Luck, Cock Lock, Henny
Penny and Chicken Licken.
As they were going along
they met Foxy Woxy.

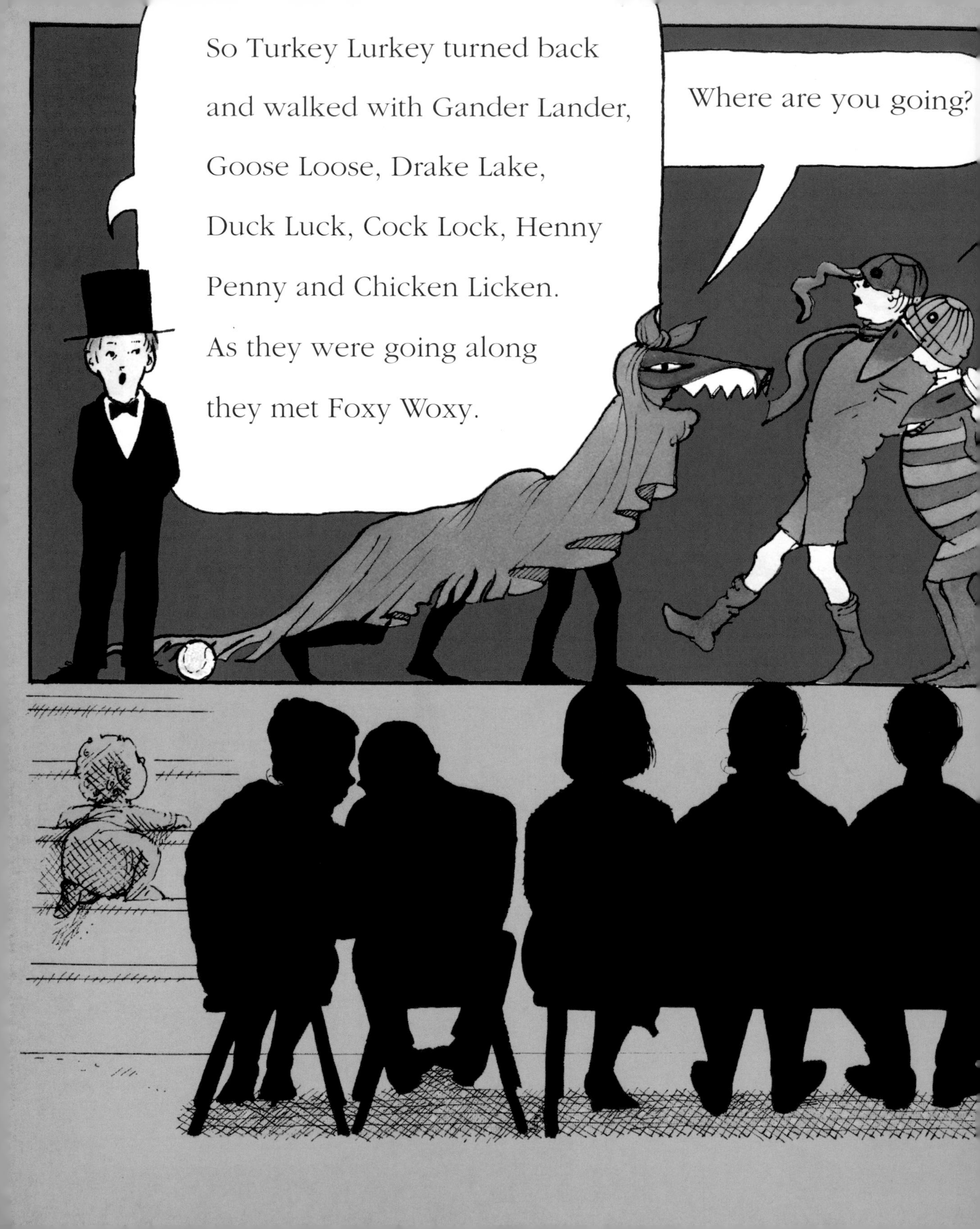

Chicken Licken went to the woods
and the sky fell
on her poor little head.
Now we are going to tell the king.

Foxy Woxy took them

into the fox's hole.

He and his young ones

soon ate up poor Chicken Licken,

Henny Penny, Cock Lock, Duck Luck,

Drake Lake, Goose Loose,

Gander Lander and Turkey Lurkey.

So they never saw the king

and they never told him

that the sky had fallen.

Read it again

School play

You can use the front page picture of the stage, the curtains and the audience to talk about the fact that this is the story of a school play. You may like to use different voices for the characters as you read and point to whoever is speaking.

> So Chicken Licken turned back and met Henny Penny.

> *I am going to the woods …*

> OH, HENNY PENNY, DON'T GO!

> So Henny Penny turned back and met Cock Lock.

Children can tell the story of the baby which is told in the pictures, not in words. Look at each picture in turn and describe together what happens. You could tell stories about your child as a baby, using photographs, and make a photograph book about the first adventures you both remember.

Play a part

Once this story has been read aloud several times, you could invite your child to read a part. A good way to start would be with the speech bubble in the middle of each page: "I am going to the woods for some food". Your child could be encouraged to put on different voices to suit each character.

I'm Foxy Woxy and I've got a DEEP voice.

Different journeys

This is a story where one character sets off on a journey and meets others along the way. Children can make up their own story using the same pattern about a journey to the park, the shops or school where they meet friends, animals or story characters. You could write it down together in a book with pictures of all the different characters.

One day Katey Latey went to the park and a conker fell on her poor little head Oh no! The moon has fallen I will go and tell the king So Katey Latey turned back and met Jack Sack

Make a puppet

Together try making simple sock puppets, paper masks or hats for each character. Children can use these to act out the story with friends, brothers or sisters, with you or on their own.

They can also use them to make up their own stories about the characters.

Reading Together

The *Reading Together* series is divided into four levels – starting with red, then on to yellow, blue and finally green. The six books in each level offer children varied experiences of reading. There are stories, poems, rhymes and songs, traditional tales and information books to choose from.

Accompanying the series is a Parents' Handbook, which looks at all the different ways children learn to read and explains how *your* help can really make a difference!